WORK
AND OTHER
OCCUPATIONAL
HAZARDS

Selected by **Bruce Lansky**

W0006474

Meadowbrook Press
Distributed by Simon & Schuster
New York

Library of Congress Cataloging-in-Publication Data
Work and other occupational hazards: the best quotes, quips, rhymes & cartoons about work / selected by
    Bruce Lansky.
        p. cm.
    ISBN 0-88166-309-5 (Meadowbrook) — ISBN 0-671-02387-X (Simon & Schuster)
    1. Work—Quotations, maxims, etc. 2. Work—Humor. I. Lansky, Bruce.
    PN6084.W67W67   1998
    331'.02'07—dc21
                                                                    98-3186
                                                                    CIP

Editor: Bruce Lansky
Coordinating Editors: David Cox and Heather Hooper
Production Manager: Joe Gagne
Production Assistant: Danielle White
Cover Art: Jack Lindstrom

Quotation: pp. 12-13 Exerpts from *Lexicon of Intentionally Ambiguous Recommendations (L.I.A.R.)*. Second
Edition. © 1998 by Robert Thornton. Reprinted with permission of Almus Publications.

Poem: pp. 70 © by Richard Armour. Reprinted from *Light Year '87* by permission of Bits Press.

Published by Meadowbrook Press, 5451 Smetana Drive, Minnetonka, Minnesota 55343

BOOK TRADE DISTRIBUTION by Simon & Schuster, a division of Simon and Schuster, Inc., 1230 Avenue of the
Americas, New York, NY 10020

02 01 00 99 98   10 9 8 7 6 5 4 3 2 1

Printed in the United States of America

CONTENTS

ACKNOWLEDGMENTS

We would like to thank the individuals
who served on a reading panel for this project:

Polly Andersen, David W. Arbogast, Ann Ballard, Michael N. Ballard,
Ken Bastien, Anne Boyd, Dianne C. Bryan, Olga Cossi, Holly Davis,
Dick Hayman, Larry Holgerson, Janet F. Hoover, Kenneth Horton,
Arleta Little, Jean H. Marvin, Barbara Merchant, Julie Mieseler,
Sheryl Nelms, Jens Oertel, Liya Lev Oertel, Elizabeth Paterra,
Reggie Platzer, Jerry Rosen, Phil Salzer, Lawerence Schimel,
Rosemary J. Schmidt, Mary Scott, Elizabeth A. Thompson,
Timothy Tocher, Dan Verdick, Evelyn A. Wade, Andrew J. Welch,
David Wexler, and George R. Winsor

Thank you to Almus Publications for allowing us to use an excerpt
from the *Lexicon of Intentionally Ambiguous Recommendations*
(L.I.A.R.) Second Edition. © 1998 by Robert J. Thornton.

INTRODUCTION

The old joke about work was: "Work is fascinating. I could sit and watch it for hours." And while many people still share this sentiment, others find they can relate even more to jokes about stupid work rules, boring meetings, do-nothing committees, and high-priced consultants.

This book reflects the best contemporary humor about work and making money from a wide range of sources: from Scott Adams and Woody Allen to Alfred E. Neuman and his most famous disciple, Ronald Reagan. It includes quotes, jokes, poems, and cartoons—all artfully arranged to provide at least one smile or chuckle on every spread. Open this book at random to any page (excluding, of course, the table of contents or the index) and see if that's not true.

This book can help you turn any meeting into a very humorous occasion. And, it's a great way to introduce a recent graduate or new employee to work and other occupational hazards.

Bruce Lansky

Corporation: An ingenious device for obtaining individual profit without individual responsibility.
—*Ambrose Bierce*

Business is the art of extracting money from another man's pocket without resorting to violence.
—*Max Amsterdam*

A criminal is a person with predatory instincts without sufficient capital to form a corporation.
—*Howard Scott*

Socialism . . . If you have two cows, you give your neighbor one.

Communism . . . If you have two cows, you give them to the government and the government gives you some milk.

Fascism . . . If you have two cows, you keep the cows and give the milk to the government and the government then sells you some of the milk.

New-Dealism . . . If you have two cows, you shoot one and milk the other and then pour the milk down the drain.

Nazism . . . If you have two cows, the government shoots you and keeps the cows.

Capitalism . . . If you have two cows, you sell one and buy a bull.

—*Anonymous*

My folks are immigrants and they fell under the spell of the American legend that the streets were paved with gold. When Papa got here he found out three things: 1) The streets were not paved with gold. 2) The streets were not paved at all. 3) He was supposed to do the paving.
—Sam Levenson

Nobody talks more of free enterprise and competition and of the best man winning than the man who inherited his father's store or farm.
—C. Wright Mills

At a testimonial dinner in his honor, a wealthy businessman gave an emotional speech. "When I came to this city fifty years ago," he said, "I had no car, my only suit was on my back, the soles of my shoes were thin, and I carried all my possessions in a paper bag." After dinner, a young man nervously approached. "Sir, I really admire your accomplishments. Tell me, after all these years, do you still remember what you carried in the brown paper bag?" "Sure, son," he said. "I had $300,000 in cash and $500,000 in negotiable securities."

—Anonymous

"*As one citizen to another, Mr. Crutchfield, I suggest you make a run for the border.*"

When there is a public outcry to cut the deadwood and fat from any government bureaucracy, it is the deadwood and fat that *does* the cutting.

—*John T. Margary*

Organized crime in America takes in over forty billion dollars a year. This is quite a profitable sum, especially when one considers that the mafia spends very little for office supplies.

—*Woody Allen*

7

An applicant for a job with the federal government was filling out an application form. He came to this question: "Do you favor the overthrow of the United States government by force, subversion, or violence?" Thinking it was a multiple-choice question, he checked "violence."

—*Anonymous*

The closest anyone ever comes to perfection is on the job-application form.

—*Anonymous*

Wanted: Circus clown with experience. Serious applicants only.

—*Help-Wanted Ad*

Experience is the name everyone gives
to their mistakes.
—*Oscar Wilde*

Experience is what enables you to recognize a
mistake when you make it again.
—*Earl Wilson*

When a person with money meets a person with
experience, the person with the experience winds
up with the money and the person with the
money winds up with the experience.
—*Harvey Mackay*

Applicant: Does this company have any death benefits?

Interviewer: Yes, it does. When you die you don't have to come to work anymore.

—Anonymous

Interviewer: This job requires someone who is very responsible.

Applicant: That's me. At my last seven jobs, whenever anything went wrong, I was responsible.

—Anonymous

*"According to your résumé you're my oldest son . . .
could you elaborate on that?"*

INTENTIONALLY AMBIGUOUS JOB RECOMMENDATIONS

Recommendation	Meaning
She was always high in my opinion.	She was often seen smoking a joint.
While he worked with us he was given numerous citations.	He was arrested many times.
I would say that his real talent is getting wasted at his current job.	He gets bombed regularly.
I am pleased to say that this candidate is a former colleague of mine.	I can't tell you how happy I am that she left our firm.

Recommendation

You simply won't believe
this woman's credentials.

He would always ask if
there was anything he
could do.

You will never catch him
asleep on the job.

He doesn't know the
meaning of the word
quit.

Meaning

She faked most of
her résumé.

We were always
wondering too.

He's too crafty to
get caught.

He can't spell it,
either.

—Robert Thornton

If you pay peanuts, you get monkeys.
—*James Goldsmith*

The less important you are in the table of organization, the more you'll be missed if you don't turn up for work.
—*Bill Vaughan*

Be awful nice to 'em going up, because you're gonna meet 'em all comin' down.
—*Jimmy Durante*

There ain't no rules around here!
We're trying to accomplish something!
—*Thomas Edison*

Notice:

This department requires no physical fitness
program: everyone gets enough exercise jumping
to conclusions, flying off the handle, running
down the boss, knifing friends in the back,
dodging responsibility, and pushing their luck.
—*Anonymous*

RULES OF THE OFFICE

If it rings, put it on hold;
If it clanks, call the repairman;
If it whistles, ignore it;
If it's a friend, take a break;
If it's the boss, look busy;
If it talks, take notes;
If it's handwritten, type it;
If it's typed, copy it;
If it's copied, file it;
If it's Friday, forget it!
—David Broome

To err is human, but it is against
company policy.
—*Anonymous*

Our Office Dress Code:
Cover your butt at all times.
—*Anonymous*

It doesn't have to make sense;
it's company policy!
—*Tom LaFleur*

18

If you get a good parking spot,
you've probably shown up on the wrong day.
—*Sam Liebman*

Do you know what it means to go to an office
where you are respected as a human being;
where your opinion is appreciated; where your
superiors treat you as an equal? It means
you've gone to the wrong office.
—*Anonymous*

If you have a job without aggravations,
you don't have a job.
—*Malcolm Forbes*

When a fellow says it isn't the money but the principle of the thing, it's the money.
—*Kin Hubbard*

When you say that you agree to a thing in principle, you mean that you have not the slightest intention of carrying it out in practice.
—*Bismarck*

The man who says he is willing to meet you halfway is usually a poor judge of distance.
—*Laurence J. Peter*

The man who can smile when things go wrong
has thought of someone he can blame it on.
—*Arthur Bloch*

I have my faults. But being wrong
ain't one of them.
—*Jimmy Hoffa*

I'm always open to honest criticism
from you judgmental creeps.
—*Robert Altman*

It's difficult to soar with eagles
when you work with turkeys.
—*Anonymous*

I have noticed that the people who are late
are often so much jollier than the people who
have to wait for them.
—*E.V. Lucas*

Ever notice that the people who say,
"That's the way the ball bounces" are usually
the ones who dropped it?
—*Jeff Rovin*

ENGINEER'S DICTIONARY

Major Technological Breakthrough:
Back to the drawing board.

Developed after Years of Intensive Research:
It was discovered by accident.

Project Slightly Behind Original Schedule
Due to Unforeseen Difficulties:
We are working on something else.

Preliminary Operational Tests Were Inconclusive:
The darn thing blew up when we threw the
switch.

Test Results Were Extremely Gratifying:
It works and are we surprised!!!

The Entire Concept Will Have to Be Abandoned:
The only guy who understood the thing quit.

*Modifications Are Under Way to Correct
Certain Minor Difficulties:*
We threw the whole thing out and are
starting from scratch.
—Alan Dundes and Carl R. Pagter

There are three kinds of employees:
those who make things happen;
those who watch things happen;
and those who have no idea at all
what is happening.
—*Anonymous*

The brain is a wonderful organ; it starts working
the moment you get up in the morning and does
not stop until you get into the office.
—*Robert Frost*

A memorandum is written not to inform the
reader but to protect the writer.
—*Dean Acheson*

Secretaries always go to Heaven . . .
God is afraid of what the devil could
accomplish if he had a good secretary.
—*Anonymous*

He and I had an office so tiny that an inch
smaller and it would have been adultery.
—*Dorothy Parker*

If I learned to type, I never would have made
brigadier general.
—*Elizabeth Hoisington*

"Here's a great idea. It's from me."

Executive ability
Is quite an art, it's true;
The art of taking credit for
The work that others do.
    —*Charles Ghigna*

Ever stop to think that BOSS spelled
backwards is double S-O-B?
—*Anonymous*

If you can't say something nice—
you have management potential.
—*Anonymous*

Tell your boss what you think of him,
and the truth shall set you free.
—*Anonymous*

A leader should not get too far in front of his troops or he will get shot in the ass.
—*Senator Joseph S. Clark*

The secret of managing is to keep the guys who hate you away from the guys who are undecided.
—*Casey Stengel*

Leadership appears to be the art of getting others to want to do something you are convinced should be done.
—*Vance Packard*

In a hierarchy, every employee tends to rise
to his level of incompetence.
—*Laurence J. Peter*

Fortunately for us, Japan is opening its first
business school in the near future.
This is likely to produce a measurable drop
in Japanese productivity.
—*Felix Rohatyn*

There's always room at the top—
after the investigation.
—*Oliver Herford*

Nothing is so embarrassing as watching your boss do something you assured him couldn't be done.

—*Earl Wilson*

Manager: This makes five times this week I've had to reprimand you. What do you have to say for yourself?

Clerk: Thank God it's Friday.

—*Anonymous*

Powerful men often succeed through the help of their wives. Powerful women only succeed in spite of their husbands.
—*Linda Lee Potter*

If a man mulls over a decision, they say, "He's weighing the options." If a woman *does* it, they say, "She can't make up her mind."
—*Barbara Proctor*

If women can sleep their way to the top, how come they aren't there?
—*Ellen Goodman*

If you want anything said, ask a man. If you want anything done, ask a woman.
—Margaret Thatcher

Whatever women do they must do twice as well as men to be thought half as good. Luckily, this is not difficult.
—Charlotte Whitton

If men can run the world, why can't they stop wearing neckties? How intelligent is it to start the day by tying a little noose around your neck?
—Linda Ellerbee

Make three correct guesses consecutively and you will establish a reputation as an expert.
—*Laurence J. Peter*

One accurate measurement is worth a thousand expert opinions.
—*Grace Murray Hopper*

(An expert is) somebody who is more than fifty miles from home, has no responsibility for implementing the advice he gives, and shows slides.
—*Edwin Meese*

"Thank God! A panel of experts!"

A consultant is a man who knows 147 ways to make love, but doesn't know any women.
—*Anonymous*

A consultant is someone who saves his client almost enough to pay his fee.
—*Arnold H. Glasow*

All too many consultants, when asked, "What is two and two?" respond, "What did you have in mind?"
—*Norman R. Augustine*

If all economists were laid end to end,
they would not reach a conclusion.
—*George Bernard Shaw*

A study of economics usually reveals that
the best time to buy anything is last year.
—*Marty Allen*

What is a committee? A group of the unwilling, picked from the unfit, to do the unnecessary.
—Richard Harkness

A conference is a gathering of important people who singly can do nothing, but together can decide that nothing can be done.
—Fred Allen

Meetings are indispensable when you don't want to do anything.
—John Kenneth Galbraith

A decision is what a man makes when he can't find anybody to serve on a committee.
—*Fletcher Knebel*

Committees have become so important nowadays that subcommittees have to be appointed to do the work.
—*Laurence J. Peter*

To get something done, a committee should consist of no more than three men, two of whom are absent.
—*Robert Copeland*

Eric & Bill

"Opposing views are welcome, but not from any of you."

Chairman: Right, let's vote on the recommendation. All those against, raise their hands and say, "I resign."

—*Anonymous*

If Columbus had had an advisory committee,
he would probably still be at the dock.
—*Arthur Goldberg*

Outside of traffic, there is nothing that has
held this country back as much as committees.
—*Will Rogers*

If you want to kill any idea in the world,
get a committee working on it.
—*Charles F. Kettering*

Having served on various committees,
I have drawn up a list of rules:

1) Never arrive on time: this stamps
you as a beginner.

2) Don't say anything until the meeting
is over: this stamps you as being wise.

3) Be as vague as possible: this avoids
irritating others.

4) When in doubt, suggest that a
subcommittee be appointed.

5) Be the first to move for adjournment:
this will make you popular—
it's what everyone is waiting for.
    —*Harry Chapman*

Opportunities are usually disguised as hard work, so most people don't recognize them.
—*Ann Landers*

The reason worry kills more people than work is that more people worry than work.
—*Robert Frost*

It's true that hard work never killed anybody, but I figure—why take the chance?
—*Ronald Reagan*

I like work; it fascinates me.
I can sit and look at it for hours.
—*Jerome K. Jerome*

If people really liked to work, we'd still be
plowing the land with sticks and transporting
goods on our backs.
—*William Feather*

If hard work were such a wonderful thing, surely
the rich would have kept it all to themselves.
—*Lane Kirkland*

By working faithfully eight hours a day,
you may eventually get to be a boss
and work twelve hours a day.
—*Robert Frost*

The difference between a job and a career is the
difference between forty and sixty hours a week.
—*Robert Frost*

Being in your own business is working eighty
hours a week so that you can avoid working
forty hours a week for someone else.
—*Ramona E. F. Arnett*

Doing a good job here is like wetting your pants in a dark suit—it gives you a warm feeling, but nobody notices.

—*Anonymous*

When I have a tough job in the plant and can't find an easy way to do it, I have a lazy man put on it. He'll find an easy way to do it in ten days. Then we adopt that method.

—*Clarence E. Bleicher*

Anyone can do any amount of work, provided it isn't the work he is supposed to be doing at that moment.

—*Robert Benchley*

Because of his ongoing ability to increase office productivity, the "Employee of the Month" award again goes to Mr. Coffee.

—*Randy Glasbergen*

"The coffeemaker is broken."

When you come in late for work, everybody notices; when you work late, nobody notices.
—*Raymond F. Elsner*

The only thing wrong with getting to work on time, is that it makes for a really long day!
—*Tom LaFleur*

Tomorrow is often the busiest day of the week.
—*Spanish Proverb*

No man does as much today as he is going
to do tomorrow.
—*Bob Edwards*

Work is the greatest thing in the world, so we
should always save some of it for tomorrow.
—*Don Herold*

According to the latest statistics, there are
five million Americans who aren't working.
And there are plenty more if you count
the ones with jobs.
—*Anonymous*

It is impossible to enjoy idling unless
there is plenty of work to do.
—*Jerome K. Jerome*

Ninety-eight percent of the adults in this country are decent, hard-working Americans. It's the other lousy two percent that get all the publicity. But then—we elected them.
—*Lily Tomlin*

There are an enormous number of managers who have retired on the job.
—*Peter Drucker*

Applicant: How many people work at this office?
Interviewer: About half of them.
—*Fred Metcalf*

The quickest way to get your child's attention is to lay your evening work out on your desk and announce that you cannot be disturbed.
—*Bruce Lansky*

Before I had kids I went home after work to rest. Now I go to work to rest.
—*Simon Ruddell*

Of course I came to work sick—you don't think
I'd waste a day at home feeling like this!
—*Tom LaFleur*

I've used up all my sick days, so I'm calling in
dead tomorrow!
—*Tom LaFleur*

The downside of going on a two-week vacation.

Nothing lasts forever, except the day before
you start your vacation.

—*Anonymous*

Vacation is time off to remind employees that
the business can get along without them.

—*Earl Wilson*

Money is something you got to make
in case you don't die.
—*Max Asnas*

Money frees you from doing things
you dislike. Since I dislike doing nearly
everything, money is handy.
—*Groucho Marx*

If you don't want to work, you have to work
to earn enough money so that you won't
have to work.
—*Ogden Nash*

Money buys everything except love, personality,
freedom, immortality, silence, peace.
—*Carl Sandburg*

Money really isn't everything. If it was, what
would we buy with it?
—*Tom Wilson*

I don't want money. It is only people who pay
their bills who want that, and I never pay mine.
—*Oscar Wilde*

Credit: A person who can't pay,
gets another person who can't pay,
to guarantee that he can pay.
—*Charles Dickens*

Creditors have better memories than debtors.
—*Benjamin Franklin*

Live within your income,
even if you have to borrow to do it.
—*Josh Billings*

Drive-in banks were invented so that
automobiles could visit their real owners.
—*Anonymous*

There's only one problem with buying something
on credit. By the time you're really sick of
something, you finally own it.
—*Anonymous*

If you think nobody cares if you're alive,
try missing a couple of car payments.
—*Earl Wilson*

The thrift industry is really in terrible shape. It has reached the point where if you buy a toaster, you get a free savings and loan.
—*Senator Lloyd Bentsen*

Finance is the art of passing money from hand to hand until it finally disappears.
—*Robert W. Sarnoff*

If only God would give me some clear sign! Like making a deposit in my name in a Swiss bank account.
—*Woody Allen*

Nowadays, people can be divided into three classes—the Haves, the Have-Nots, and the Have-Not-Paid-for-What-They-Haves.
—*Earl Wilson*

The reason most of us don't live within our income is that we don't consider that living.
—*Joe Moore*

In God we trust, all others pay cash.
—*Sign used in retail stores during the Depression*

A bank is a place where they lend you
an umbrella in fair weather and ask for it back
when it begins to rain.
—*Robert Frost*

I don't have a bank account because I don't
know my mother's maiden name.
—*Paula Poundstone*

A banker is a person who is willing to make a
loan if you present sufficient evidence
to show you don't need it.
—*Herbert V. Prochnow*

*"Gosh, Mr. Birnbaum . . . I thought you knew about
our penalty for early withdrawal."*

It's called "cold cash" because it's never in your pocket long enough to get warm.
—*Jeff Rovin*

Why is there always so much month left at the end of the money?
—*Anonymous*

Save a little money each month
and at the end of the year
you'll be surprised at how little you have.
—*Ernest Haskins*

Saving is a very fine thing, especially when your parents have done it for you.
—*Winston Churchill*

You can't have everything.
Where would you put it?
—*Steven Wright*

They say you can't take it with you.
I can't even afford to go.
—*Milton Berle*

MONEY

That money talks
I'll not deny,
I heard it once;
It said, "Good-bye."
—*Richard Armour*

Two can live as cheap as one;
I guess I always knew it.
But now it takes the two of us
To earn enough to do it.
  —Evelyn Amuedo Wade

Sadly, the boss said to the employee who was leaving, "We'll never be able to replace you, especially at the salary we've been paying you."
—*Milton Berle*

"Now remember, Royce—your salary is confidential and should not be discussed with anyone else in the company," the manager instructed.

"Oh, don't worry, Ms. Amorelli," the new employee assured her. "I'm just as ashamed of it as you are."
—*Anonymous*

The only difference between a pigeon and the American farmer today is that a pigeon can still make a deposit on a John Deere.
—*James Allen Hightower*

Inflation means that your money won't buy as much today as it did when you didn't have any.
—*Anonymous*

Work is the price you pay for money.
—*Anonymous*

"Some cost-of-living increase. Evidently they don't expect me to live much longer."

I hated to go in and ask my boss for a raise the
other day, but my kids found out that other
kids eat three times a day.
—*Milton Berle*

A boss told his workers that he was planning
a salary raise. One employee asked,
"When does it become effective?"
The boss answered, "As soon as you do."
—*Milton Berle*

A fool and his money are soon parted.
What I want to know is how they got
together in the first place.
—*Cyril Fletcher*

There was a time when a fool and his
money were soon parted, but now
it happens to everybody.
—*Adlai E. Stevenson*

Some people who go into business for
themselves have more money than brains.
But not for long.
—*Anonymous*

Now I'm in real trouble. First, my laundry called
and said they lost my shirt. Then my broker
said the same thing.
—*Leopold Fechtner*

I started out with nothing.
I still have most of it.
—*Michael Davis*

Bargain: Something you can't use
at a price you can't resist.
—*Franklin P. Jones*

The first person to make a mountain out of a molehill was a real-estate agent.
—*Anonymous*

Whoever uses the term "dirt cheap" probably hasn't bought any real estate recently.
—*D.O. Flynn*

When Joe Louis was asked who had hit him the hardest during his boxing career, he replied, "That's easy—Uncle Sam!"
—*Anonymous*

It is getting harder and harder to support the government in the style to which it has become accustomed.
—*Anonymous*

I wouldn't mind paying taxes—if I knew they were going to a friendly country.
—*Dick Gregory*

"He owed a lot of back taxes."

There's nothing wrong with the younger
generation that becoming taxpayers
won't cure.
—*Thomas LaMance*

Today it takes more brains and effort to
make out the income-tax form than it does
to make the income.
—*Alfred E. Neuman*

The taxpayer—that's someone who works
for the federal government but doesn't
have to take a civil service exam.
—*Ronald Reagan*

Once, a man with an alligator walked into a pub and
asked the bartender, "Do you serve IRS agents here?"
"Sure do," the bartender replied.
"Good, give me a beer," said the man,
"and my gator'll have an IRS agent."
—Anonymous

What is the difference between a taxidermist
and a tax collector? The taxidermist takes
only your skin.
—Mark Twain

Lottery: A tax on people who are bad at math.
—Anonymous

The wages of sin are unreported.
—Anonymous

The guy who invented the first wheel was an idiot. The guy who invented the other three, he was the genius.

—*Sid Caesar*

Fortunately the wheel was invented before the car, otherwise the scraping noise would have been terrible!

—*Laurence J. Peter*

The factory of the future will have only two employees—a man and a dog. The man will be there to feed the dog. The dog will be there to keep the man from touching the equipment.
—*Warren G. Bennis*

My father worked for the same firm for twelve years. They fired him. They replaced him with a tiny gadget this big. It does everything that my father does, only much better. The depressing thing is—my mother ran out and bought one.
—*Woody Allen*

In the computer world, hardware is anything you can hit with a hammer, and software is what you can only curse at.

—*Anonymous*

Computers come in two varieties:
the prototype and the obsolete.

—*Anonymous*

Monday was so depressing that even the computers were down.

—*Timothy Tocher*

Nowadays the only "windows" you can open in an office building were created by Bill Gates.
—*Timothy Tocher*

Computers are useless.
They can only give you answers.
—*Pablo Picasso*

The computer is a great invention. There are just as many mistakes as ever. But they are nobody's fault.
—*Anonymous*

"The computer system is down again."

We are not ready for any unforeseen event
that may or may not occur.
—*Dan Quayle*

The reason that everybody likes planning
is that nobody has to do anything.
—*Jerry Brown*

For every problem there is a solution that is
simple, neat, and wrong.
—*H. L. Mencken*

Go ahead and destroy those old files,
but make copies of them first.
—*Samuel Goldwyn*

Why is it that there is never enough time
to do a job right, but always enough time
to do it over?
—*Anonymous*

It is impossible to make anything foolproof,
because fools are so ingenious.
—*Anonymous*

Get your facts straight first, then you can
distort them as you please.
—*Mark Twain*

There are three kinds of lies:
lies, damned lies, and statistics.
—*Benjamin Disraeli*

Torture the data long enough
and it will tell you whatever you want.
—*Anonymous*

If at first you don't succeed, try, try again. Then quit. There's no use being a damn fool about it.
—*W.C. Fields*

If at first you *do* succeed— try to hide your astonishment.
—*Harry F. Banks*

Sometimes I worry about being a success in a mediocre world.
—*Lily Tomlin*

SUBTLE SIGNS THE COMPANY MAY BE DOWNSIZING

The traditional Christmas Turkey consists of an egg and hatching instructions.

You call in sick and personnel says, "That's the spirit!"

You notice the employee out-placement program consists of a copy of the want ads and a lottery ticket.

Your new computer terminal says "Fisher Price" on it.

The vacation schedule has a notation: "If you feel like staying longer, go for it!"

Management is passing out "Two-Week Pins" honoring long-term employees.

At quitting time no one says, "See you tomorrow!"

You complain to personnel about longer hours, lower pay, less help, lack of benefits, and they respond, "Yeah, so what's your point?"

—*Marion Foust*

A former executive of a company that had been taken over in a corporate merger gave this description of what happened to his company's executive personnel: "We got the mushroom treatment. Right after the acquisition, we were left in the dark. Then they covered us with manure. Then they cultivated us. After that they let us stew awhile. Finally, they canned us."

—*Isadore Barmash*

DILBERT © United Features Syndicate. Reprinted by Permission

**If you aren't fired with enthusiasm,
you will be fired with enthusiasm.**
—*Vince Lombardi*

**My unemployed brother-in-law gave up his job
because of illness. His boss got sick of him.**
—*Henry Youngman*

A lot of fellows nowadays have a B.A., M.D., or Ph.D. Unfortunately, they don't have a J.O.B.
—*Fats Domino*

The trouble with unemployment is that the minute you wake up in the morning you're on the job.
—*Slappy White*

A computer salesman dies and meets St. Peter at the Pearly Gates. St. Peter tells the salesman he can choose between heaven and hell. First, he shows the man heaven; people in white robes playing harps and floating around. "Dull," says the salesman. Next, St. Peter shows him hell: toga parties, good food and wine, and people looking as though they're having a fine time. "I'll take hell," he says. He enters the gates of hell and is immediately set upon by demons who poke him with pitchforks. "Hey," the salesman demands as Satan walks past, "what happened to the party I saw going on?" "Ah," Satan replies. "You must have seen our demo."

—*Anonymous*

The easiest job in the world has to be a coroner. Surgery on dead people. What's the worst that can happen? If it all goes wrong . . . maybe you get a pulse.
—*Dennis Miller*

A good rule of thumb is that if you've made it to thirty-five and your job still requires you to wear a name tag, you've probably made a serious vocational error.
—*Dennis Miller*

I had a boring office job. I cleaned the windows in the envelopes.
—*Rita Rudner*

The trouble with the rat race is that
even if you win, you're still a rat.
—*Lily Tomlin*

It's just a job. Grass grows, birds fly, waves
pound the sand. I beat people up.
—*Muhammad Ali*

Work is all right for killing time, son,
but it's no way to make a living.
—*Bret Maverick*

INDEX

For Better And For Worse
Revised Edition
Selected by Bruce Lansky

This entertaining collection of wit and wisdom about marriage is an ideal gift for wedding showers, bachelor or bachelorette parties, anniversaries, or birthdays. Roseanne, Jerry Seinfeld, Rita Rudner, Bill Cosby, Richard Lewis, and many other notables are quoted at their hilarious best! Illustrated with 17 cartoons.

Order #4000

Familiarity Breeds Children
Revised Edition
Selected by Bruce Lansky

Lansky has created a humor book for parents that will delight and revive them. This collection is a treasury of the most outrageous and clever quotes and cartoons about raising children by world-class comedians and humorists, including Roseanne, Erma Bombeck, Bill Cosby, Dave Barry, Mark Twain, Fran Lebowitz, and others. Illustrated with 18 cartoons.

Order #4015

Lovesick

Selected by Bruce Lansky

Here is a collection of the funniest quotes and cartoons about America's favorite pastimes: love and sex. This is the perfect gift for Valentine's Day, wedding showers, birthdays, and anniversaries. It includes quotes from well-known humorists such as Tim Allen, Garry Shandling, Richard Lewis, Rodney Dangerfield, and Mae West.

Order #4045

Age Happens

Selected by Bruce Lansky

Here is a compilation of the funniest things ever said about growing older by the most insightful wits of all time: Ellen DeGeneres, Garrison Keillor, Bill Cosby, and many more! This book includes 15 cartoons by some of *The New Yorker's* most popular cartoonists.

Order #4025

Golf: It's Just a Game!

Selected by Bruce Lansky

Bruce Lansky has hit a hole-in-one with this collection of clever golf quotes from such devotees of the game as Lee Trevino, Harvey Penick, Yogi Berra, Henry Beard, Gerald Ford, Bob Hope, and many, many more. Illustrated with some of the funniest cartoons ever to appear in *Golf Digest* and *Playboy*.

Order #4035

Order Form

Qty.	Title	Author	Order #	Unit Cost (U.S. $)	Total
	Age Happens	Lansky, B.	4025	$7.00	
	Dads Say the Dumbest Things!	Lansky/Jones	4220	$6.00	
	Familiarity Breeds Children	Lansky, B.	4015	$7.00	
	For Better And For Worse	Lansky, B.	4000	$7.00	
	Golf: It's Just a Game!	Lansky, B.	4035	$7.00	
	Grandma Knows Best	McBride, M.	4009	$7.00	
	How to Line Up Your Fourth Putt	Rusher, B.	4075	$7.00	
	How to Survive Your 40th Birthday	Dodds, B.	4260	$6.00	
	Joy of Friendship	Scotellaro, R.	3506	$7.00	
	Joy of Grandparenting	Sherins/Holleman	3502	$7.00	
	Joy of Marriage	Dodds, M. & B.	3504	$7.00	
	Joy of Parenthood	Blaustone, J.	3500	$7.00	
	Joy of Sisters	Brown, K.	3508	$7.00	
	Lovesick	Lansky, B.	4045	$7.00	
	Moms Say the Funniest Things!	Lansky, B.	4280	$6.00	
	Work and Other Occupational Hazards	Lansky, B.	4016	$7.00	
				Subtotal	
			Shipping and Handling (see below)		
			MN residents add 6.5% sales tax		
				Total	

YES! Please send me the books indicated above. Add $2.00 shipping and handling for the first book and 50¢ for each additional book. Add $2.50 to total for books shipped to Canada. Overseas postage will be billed. Allow up to four weeks for delivery. Send check or money order payable to Meadowbrook Press. No cash or COD's, please. Prices subject to change without notice. **Quantity discounts available upon request.**

Send book(s) to:

Name_____ Address _____

City_____ State ___ Zip _____ Telephone (____) _____

P.O. number (if necessary) _____

Payment via:

❏ Check or money order payable to Meadowbrook Press   Amount enclosed $ _____

❏ Visa ❏ MasterCard (for orders over $10.00 only)

Account # _____ Signature _____ Exp. Date _____

A *FREE* Meadowbrook Press catalog is available upon request.

Mail to: Meadowbrook Press, 5451 Smetana Drive, Minnetonka, MN 55343

Phone (612) 930-1100   Toll-Free 1-800-338-2232   Fax (612) 930-1940